WITH WORDS

Young Writers' 16th Annual Poetry Competition

It is feeling and force of imagination that make us eloquent.

How can I not dream while writing? The blank page gives a right to dream.

Northamptonshire
Edited by Donna Samworth

Young Writers

First published in Great Britain in 2007 by:
Young Writers
Remus House
Coltsfoot Drive
Peterborough
PE2 9JX
Telephone: 01733 890066
Website: www.youngwriters.co.uk

All Rights Reserved

© Copyright Contributors 2007

SB ISBN 978-1 84431 138 5

Foreword

This year, the Young Writers' *Away With Words* competition proudly presents a showcase of the best poetic talent selected from thousands of up-and-coming writers nationwide.

Young Writers was established in 1991 to promote the reading and writing of poetry within schools and to the young of today. Our books nurture and inspire confidence in the ability of young writers and provide a snapshot of poems written in schools and at home by budding poets of the future.

The thought, effort, imagination and hard work put into each poem impressed us all and the task of selecting poems was a difficult but nevertheless enjoyable experience.

We hope you are as pleased as we are with the final selection and that you and your family continue to be entertained with *Away With Words Northamptonshire* for many years to come.

Contents

Guilsborough School

Thomas Stephenson (13)	1
Daniel Brace (13)	2
Gemma Tee (13)	3
Samuel Holden (12)	4
Sheena McGee (12)	5
Holly West (13)	6
Hannah Lorimer (13)	7
Amy Clement (12)	8
Kimberley Tarry (12)	9
Emma O'Neil (13)	10
James Shaw (13)	11
Zach Goodchild (13)	12
Stephanie Langford (13)	13
Jake Watson (13)	14
Charlotte Slapper (12)	15
Mia Kinch (12)	16
Matthew Lynn (12)	17
Francesca Cave (12)	18
Matt Walters (12)	19
Victoria Garrett (12)	20
Jack O'Shea (12)	21
Rebecca Tew (12)	22
Maisie Pease (12)	23
Sam Parsons (12)	24
Thomas Oriel (13)	25
Cara Brooks (13)	26

Magdalen College School

Connor Batty (11)	27
Sophie Skinner (12)	28
Josie Isted (12)	29
Matthew Neal (12)	30
Ellen Edmondson (12)	31
Rebecca Berry (12)	32
Abigail Ogle (12)	33
Charlotte Blackwell (11)	34
Emily Collinson (11)	35
Chloe Hope (11)	36

Hayley Duncan (12)	37
Shaun Eaton (12)	38

Roade School

Tom Halder (12)	39
Charlotte Barrie (11)	40
Lucy Miller (11)	41
Georgina Baker & Sydney Marston (12)	42
Jamie Wilby (13)	43
Samantha Green (13)	44
Josh Savage (12)	45
Mette Smith (13)	46
Sean Tidder (13)	47

The Rushden Community College

Abigail Breeds (11)	48
Daniel Piper (11)	49
Amy Northwood (11)	50
Hannah Robinson (11)	51
Alice Savage (12)	52
Emma Fett (12)	53
Emily Williams (11)	54
Charlz Whitehouse (12)	55
Rachel Martin (12)	56
Emily Fensome (11)	57
Rebekah Hobbs (12)	58
Kaija McGregor (12)	59
Jodie Groves (12)	60
Thomas Alexander (11)	61
Alice Hicks (11)	62
Hollie Gordge (13)	63
Lauren Tennant (13)	64
Evangeline Maddams (13)	65
Huy Ta (12)	66
Anna Jane (12)	67
Holly Mather (13)	68
Ben Varney (12)	69
Rebecca Dix (13)	70
Terry Vickery (12)	71
Domonic Long (13)	72
Kelly Barnes (11)	73

Emma Betterton (11)	74
Jonathan Jones (12)	75
Kelsey MacGowan (11)	76
Gemma King (11)	77
Arron Scroxton (12)	78
Shannon O'Dell (11)	79
Jordan Jupp (11)	80
Traynie Atkins (12)	81
Leah Cudone (12)	82
Rya Alice Willis-Jones (11)	83
Tyler Stratford (11)	84
Paris Wills (12)	85
Adam Monger (11)	86
Jordon Brown (11)	87
Kieran Foster (11)	88
Alex Honeywood (11)	89
Jordan Thornton (12)	90
Chantelle Wornast-Humphreys (11)	91
Steven Edwards (12)	92
Brent Wills (11)	93
Peter Sanders (12)	94
Luke Davis (12)	95
Charlotte Andrews (12)	96
Hannah Samanon (11)	97
Joana Read (11)	98
Jamie-Leigh Smith (12)	99
Harry Stevenson (11)	100
Hayden Pott (11)	101
Adam Lonergan (12)	102
Sarah Hanson (12)	103
Rebecca Key (12)	104
Samuel Perry (12)	105
Travis Price (13)	106
Brittany Scott (12)	107
Katie Lawman (12)	108
Matthew White (12)	109
Jodi Wills (11)	110
Ben Warren (13)	111
Jade Scott (12)	112
Hughie Wilmshurst (16)	113
Aaron Swingler (12)	114
Daniel Todd (11)	115

Emily Dimmock (13)	116
Chloe Gallon (12)	117
Stacey Joyce (13)	118
Charlie Clayton (12)	119
Natasha Brown (12)	120
Jessica Davey (12)	121
Aaron Sinclair (13)	122
Katie Kirkup (13)	123
Justine Abbott (13)	124
Sam Loak (12)	125
Lauren Nicole Sulphur (12)	126
Luke Daniel Howe (11)	127
Leanne Denton (12)	128
Christopher Warren (12)	129
Paige Kilsby (12)	130
Cassie Reed (13)	131
Luke Rollings (13)	132
Sarah Utton (12)	133
Katie Percival (12)	134
Tom Brogan (12)	135
Joshua Dilley (13)	136
Benjamin James May (13)	137
Danielle Thomson (11)	138
Louisa Walker (12)	139
Kieran O'Connor (11)	140
Keiron Hinde (11)	141
Tom Sadler (12)	142
Jessica Norman (11)	143
Paige Kelly (11)	144
Christopher Taylor (11)	145
Frances Henman (11)	146
Hollie Wells (12)	147
Hannah Clarke (12)	148
Rhys DeBranco (11)	149

Wollaston School

Julie Bomben (11)	150
Sarah Welsby (12)	151
Charlotte Tennant (13)	152
Lewis French (11)	153
Hannah Tyrer (12)	154

Jacob Thorpe (13)	155
Wendy Mullaney (11)	156
Ryan Herdman-Grant (12)	157
Matthew West (12)	158
Sam Bolton (13)	159
Emma Roberts (13)	160
Amy Millard (11)	161
Will Smith (12)	162
Fay Wood (11)	163
Nathan Cruden (11)	164
Lauren Bandey (12)	165
Daniel Paine (11)	166
Mathew Leask (12)	167
Daniel Bottomley (12) & Shaun Turner (11)	168
Aiden Hornsby (11)	169
Daniel Womack (11)	170
April Addison (11)	172
Ben Nolan (12)	173
Thomas Williams (11)	174
Sarah Jones (12)	175
Leah Galea-Bateman (13)	176
Joanna Morton (12)	177
Kyle Adams (13)	178
Stacey Cooper (13)	179
Ashleigh Stroud (13)	180
Sarah Priscott (12)	181
Samantha Gould (12)	182

The Poems

Fugitive

As you chase me,
After I have broken free,
I could be in any tree,
Or I could have just tried to flee.

As the sky gives out lightning,
After all of my fighting,
I keep on trying,
Or I would start crying.

As the police start to crack,
After watching me not slack,
I will never look back,
Or I might take the wrong track.

As I've now escaped,
After being accused of editing a CCTV tape,
I can now life a life in a picturesque landscape.

Thomas Stephenson (13)
Guilsborough School

The Car

Rage, rage as my wheels grip the road,
Running over rabbits and even the odd toad,
Steel-cased outside, but leather comfort in,
So perfect in me, it must be a sin.
Hear me roar as my gears increase,
Keep on, keep going, chased by the police,
Exhaust spurting out fumes into the dusky sky,
Pedal to the metal and watch this Ferrari fly.
Windscreen wipers swish to clear the splattered screen,
Anything but crickets are simple to wipe clean,
Drinking fuel like blood runs in your veins,
Closed off to thunderstorm and rain.
My keys are what give me life, send a rush through my spine,
Nought to sixty in under four seconds, try and beat that time!
Lights flash on, lights flash off, I'm braking for the cops,
After my adrenaline, this is the last of my stops.

Daniel Brace (13)
Guilsborough School

The Ruined Earth

Years ago I was perfect
My seas deep pools of glistening blue
My land explosions of bright colours
And my people kind, happy and satisfied

Above, dozens of colourful birds would fly
Below, tropical snakes and lizards would writhe
And I would continuously flourish new and beautiful plants

But after millions of years of this perfect harmony
My people got too greedy
And proceeded to
Destroy
The happiness there had once been

Stunning animals wiped out, replaced by hideous machines
Called cars and planes, that roar and snarl
Ugly, grey buildings appearing everywhere, built on my fields
Little by little, demolishing my ozone layer

The perfection there had once disappeared
As if it had flown away into the universe
Hiding behind planets, or
Burnt up by stars

Leaving my once flawless plane
Now unhappy, dull and grey
In a whirl of conflict and disaster.

Gemma Tee (13)
Guilsborough School

Tree

Tree
Standing
Here doing
Nothing, never
Moving, but always
Watching, watching bombs
Dropping. Homes destroyed like
A child's block tower, their existence
Over in just a few years! Then; noise
Everywhere, music constantly throbbing
In the air: pop, swing, rock, blues, everything
Changes so quickly. People speed past; barely
Noticeable and their houses being rebuilt, large trees of brick
Shooting out the ground. They are everywhere like weeds and so
Are the cars; belching out smoke, poisoning the air and destroying
The planet, I see all of a hundred years in what seems like thirty, the
Planet going from bad to worse, I see all of this until one day:
Chop
Chop
Chop
Chop
Chop
Chop
Thud!

Samuel Holden (12)
Guilsborough School

This Is How I Live

My sore feet stumbling through the trash,
My dry mouth longing for a drink,
I'm searching for any sign of food,
In this dirty, rotten rubbish dump,
This is how I live.

> I search in the African streets,
> No food, no home, no drink, no hope,
> My stomach rumbles, crying out for food,
> My little sister cries, screaming out for her life,
> This is how I live.

I watch as other boys and girls play,
They have no worries, no hunger,
I see them go into their homes,
Knowing I will never live that dream,
This is how I live.

> My father goes out to work,
> But doesn't earn near enough
> For us to eat, to play, to enjoy our lives,
> We sleep on the streets, watching life go by,
> This is how I live.

I become desperate for a normal life,
To go to school like other kids,
Disease chases poverty,
And I know I may not live to be twenty-one,
This is how I live.

Sheena McGee (12)
Guilsborough School

Walking, Walking, Walking

Walking,
Walking,
Walking,
Through the long-lost, lonely desert,
Thirsty and exhausted,
Scared and lonely,
My bare feet pad, pad, padding through
The boiling hot sand,
The scorching sun beaming down onto
My burnt neck.
I look around me,
All I see is sand,
Lots and lots of sand.
I look a mess,
My hair all greasy,
My skin all burnt,
My mouth as dry as sandpaper.
I want to be anywhere,
Anywhere but here,
But I'm not,
I'm stuck,
Stuck here,
Walking,
Walking,
Walking.

Holly West (13)
Guilsborough School

All Alone

Emptiness
All alone
Shivers up my spine
Rubble all around me like scattered bones.

Everywhere is silent
Silent as a graveyard
Spooky and bewildered.

Pongs of mouldy meat
Linger all around.

My mouth is dry
As dry as a desert
Without months of rain
I'm as hot, hot, hot as the sun.

My mother lies dying in pain
As I search day and night
She waits for a miracle
While her heart thuds on slowly.

My sister has gone to another Earth
I feel like my world is crumbling
Crumbling underneath me.

Soon I will be alone
My heart has broken like shattered glass.

All alone.

Hannah Lorimer (13)
Guilsborough School

All Alone On This Shelf

Silence
As deserted as a desert
I am alone
On this shelf, all alone

Silence
It's as quiet as a mouse
I am alone
All my friends have left me

Silence
I am as cold as an Eskimo
I am alone
Dark and dusty with no one to talk to

Silence
I am worried, my heart beating like a drum
I am alone
Will my friends ever come back to be the way
We used to be?

Silence
All alone on this shelf.

Amy Clement (12)
Guilsborough School

War

Screams, screams getting louder and louder
Charging, running as fast as a cheetah
Get away from those barren horses

Lost as a polar bear in the desert
Scared, shaking legs turning to jelly
Wobbling, wobbling, going to fall down

Hot as a burning fire
Frightened as a man lost at sea
What is going to happen to me?

Kimberley Tarry (12)
Guilsborough School

Here I Am, Once Again

Here I am, once again,
I'm watching the world go by,
I'm turning in circles with nowhere to go,
All I can see is dead ends, dead ends, dead ends.

The world's a chessboard, all black and white,
No colour in it at all,
It's like my life - all dull and grey,
Like the sky on a stormy day.

As I stand and stare out at this world,
There's the pouring rain that never stops,
It's soaking my spirit, draining my soul,
Washing it away like mud in a river.

But still the hubbub of life goes on around me,
The kids next door screaming and shouting,
But I am not part of that, I am different,
I'm like a leaf torn from its tree.

But the most confusing thing of all,
Is although I am near someone
And although I am next to someone,
I'm always, always alone.

Emma O'Neil (13)
Guilsborough School

To Live In The Sea

As I gaze into the sea,
I wonder how it would be,
To live in the sea.
Where the fish live,
Or where the starfish sleep
And where the sharks swim.

I imagine myself as a fish,
Gliding gracefully through the water,
Swimming against the tide.
Or perhaps a shark,
Chasing my prey down,
Cutting through the water like a knife.

I could be a jellyfish,
Floating on the sea,
With the current to transport me.
Maybe a sea anemone,
Observing all around me,
Clamped to my rock.

Of all the animals in the deep,
I could be a crab,
Scuttling along the floor.
But more than that,
Above all the creatures of the sea,
I'd like to stay as me.

James Shaw (13)
Guilsborough School

Last Words

All I can hear is the blanket of terror surrounding me,
All I can feel is a shiver creeping down my spine,
All I can see is death and torture,
And all I can think about is my precious family,
All just for my religion.

There are only three things to describe war:
 W ipes out a life without a passing thought,
 A nger and devastation,
 R e-writes people's lives.

My love for Katie is like an endless tunnel,
She is the only thing that keeps me going,
Once I look into her eyes I just can't stop,
Every kiss is as precious as a diamond,
Without saying a word, you can make all the pain go away,
All along there is just one thing I want to ask . . .

And that's the last words I had from Harvey,
The rest of his letter was destroyed,
Before the war took his innocent life,
I cried, 'Why him? Why him? Why not me?'
All I can think about is what he wanted to ask.
I guess I'll never know . . .

Zach Goodchild (13)
Guilsborough School

The Last Goodbye

I miss you, Mum
The way you brushed my hair
And held my hand
You were always there
I love you

I miss you, Dad
The way you pushed me on the swing
And soothed me to sleep
You helped me with everything
I love you

I miss you, Kate
The way you picked me up when I was down
And always said 'sorry'
After pushing me around
I love you

I miss you, Woofer
The way you nibbled at my feet
And barked at the phone
You were always so sweet
I love you

Goodbye.

Stephanie Langford (13)
Guilsborough School

Last Minutes

It is the last minutes of the game.
This is my chance to get some fame!
Shall I kick the ball, or shall I drop it?
If I kick it I'll be a hero,
But if I drop it, everyone will hate me.

My friend is down in pain.
I can hear the crowd screaming my name.
'Kick it!'
'Kick it!'
What shall I do?
What shall I do?
Oh no, he's coming at me.
It's too late,
I'm on the floor,
I've been smashed
By the big man!
The fans all hate me!

Jake Watson (13)
Guilsborough School

Never Waking Up

When I lie here
My stone body won't move
I'm not sure where you are
My concrete eyes can't see you

When I lie here
I think about everything and everyone
But it's hard
Like a puzzle I don't understand

When I lie here
The ticking clock times my life
Like Sleeping Beauty
Though maybe not a happy ending

When I lie here
I feel so frustrated
Like in a prison cell all alone
I want to fly free like a bird

If I didn't lie here
I would say you mean the world to me
How you've always been there
I love you and I always will.

Charlotte Slapper (12)
Guilsborough School

In Blue's Shoes

She's arrived with breakfast
Thank the Lord, hallelujah
Hurry up, hurry up
Quick, quick, run, run
My throat has been cut
I thought you wouldn't arrive

Nearly there, nearly there
One more step, just one more
Got it, hoorah, hoorah
This food is as good as Mediterranean
All I can hear is my nose banging on the bucket
Bang, bang, bang! Smash, smash, smash!

Oh what, it's all gone
I want more, more, more, *more*
My mouth is as dry as a meadow on a beautiful summer's day
She's coming
Act normal
Nothing wrong

Oh no, grooming time
I won't stand for it
Never ever, ever, *ever*
Quick, hide
Wait, there is no place to hide
Damn it!

Mia Kinch (12)
Guilsborough School

Burning Forest

Those who they do not burn
Go into the machines that turn
After axes have hacked, gnawed and bitten
Become things upon which words are written

Animals have left the wood
To go and hide in the mud
Only to see their homes burning
And the infernal machines turning.

Matthew Lynn (12)
Guilsborough School

All Alone

Here we are, all alone
No one else exists
We are the only ones left
I don't know how it happened
I don't know why
How are we still alive?

Maybe we're not the only ones
Maybe there are still others left
We have been wandering for days
It's still all such a haze.

Francesca Cave (12)
Guilsborough School

Azza

I'm running down the wing
I'm so quick they hunt me
Like a predator and I'm the
Prey.

I'm running down the wing
Round one, round another
I'm running through them
Like a knife.

I'm running down the wing
As if I'm eating up the ground
I reach the penalty box and I go
To shoot . . .

But *thud,* I hear my leg snap - *ow,
Ow, ow!* It's a penalty, it is a penalty
To England.

But I'm out of the game and the rest
Of the season. They rush me to hospital.
As soon as I get there I ask the nurse
'What was the final score?'

The nurse says that the penalty won
England the World Cup and
Fifa has designated the goal,
Wayne Rooney scored the most
Heroic goal in the World Cup's history.

Matt Walters (12)
Guilsborough School

The Lost Bear

Here I sit all alone,
I'm so dusty,
I'm so cold.

How could she leave me?
I'm her friend,
She must think I'm just pretend.

Maybe I slipped out of her hand,
But wouldn't she have picked me up again?
I'm not that much of a pain.

The moon is shining like a diamond,
But yet it looks so cold.
The moon's made of cheese, I was once told.

I remember the time when she found me,
I was sitting on a shelf in a supermarket store.
She picked me up and hugged me, more and more.

The blistering rain is coming down harder,
That's all I can hear.
Something's on my face, is it rain or is it a tear?

Victoria Garrett (12)
Guilsborough School

Striker

Running through the centre
Flying through the wind
As fast as lightning past the players
Oblivious to everything else
The goal getting bigger, bigger, bigger

Just thinking about the goal
A win
Another trophy
The adulation

The taste of grass in my mouth
The wind rushing through my hair
The deafening sound of my glorious fans
The world feeling like it's stopped

The moment of truth
My heart pounds through my chest
I unleash a missile
Flying through the air straight for the target

The keeper soars
I see everything in slow motion
The ball arcs over the colossus
The deafening screams of the crowd as the ball crosses
The great divide

The final whistle blows
I'm so happy, bursting with joy
The opposition heartbroken and torn apart.

Jack O'Shea (12)
Guilsborough School

Green Forests

In the luscious green forest
I'm searching for food.
Drip, drip, drip
It's the juice from an apple
I want one, I want one now!
Where are they? Where could they be?

Oh! It's coming from high in that tree
I can't reach it, but I want it!
Do I carry on my search?
Do I die of hunger?
I can't decide, I don't want to die though!
But I just can't reach it.

I carry on my search
Getting strange looks because I don't belong here.
This makes me wonder
Am I meant to live in a habitat like this?
I'm sure I am, but maybe not here
I'm really not sure, however, I want to know!

I can't carry on
I realise that I don't belong here
What do I do?
Should I just leave?
Should I leave now?
What do I do?

I can't carry on, I don't feel well
Should I, as a bird, feel like this?
I go into a corner
I lie down, I close my eyes
I feel the wind brush over
The last thing I feel before I die
Is the *drip, drip, drip* from the juice of an apple.

Rebecca Tew (12)
Guilsborough School

Lost

I sit here, lonely and cold,
Watching . . . waiting,
I hear happy voices far away,
Laughing and shouting.

But nobody knows,
Nobody knows I am here,
Except for that special little girl . . .
Who left me.

The voices fade and I am alone,
Lost in the gloomy silence of the forest,
I can see a paper bag blowing in the breeze,
Like tumbleweed in a barren desert.

I remember being at home,
In a warm bed . . .
I feel my eyes fill up with tears,
One falls to the ground . . . and breaks the silence.

Maisie Pease (12)
Guilsborough School

My Son

I curl up
Against a tree
That's as dark as a stormy night,
Waiting, waiting.

I draw a tear
In the leaves
As the wind carries a whisper,
Alone, alone.

I manage a shiver
In the cold wind
That howls like a lone wolf,
Frightening, frightening.

I can't stand it
Here in this forest
As a mother cries for her lost child,
My son, my son.

Sam Parsons (12)
Guilsborough School

Love That Girl

I see you,
Walking down a one-way street,
It's going nowhere,
Away from me,

And all I want to do,
Is make you proud,
But then you had to go and say,
'My heart lies with someone else,'

I see your face
And it makes me feel warm,
Knowing that there is always hope,
But then I come crashing down once again,

Feeling this feeling inside,
That I can't describe,
Knowing it won't make a difference,
Feeling that I will always love you.

Thomas Oriel (13)
Guilsborough School

All I Can Be Is Me!

I am blind but I have perfect vision,
I am deaf but I hear everything,
I am dumb but I still understand you,
I am me and that's all I can be.

I am ill but I am forever cured,
I am poor but I own the world,
I am dying but I'll live forever,
I am lost but I will always be found.

You think I am abnormal,
You think I don't fit in,
You think I am too different,
You think I am so dim.

You do not understand me,
You do not want to know me,
You do not even like me,
But, all I can be is me.

Cara Brooks (13)
Guilsborough School

The Jock

T atty hair, in a mess
H eavy feeling in limbs, dragging him down as he celebrates
E xhaustion taking over, barely able to carry himself

J ubilant with victorious feelings, it all sinking in
O verwhelmed with a new points record, forty-one in total
C oming back into the changing rooms, the smell of deodorant in the air
K evin is 'The Jock'.

Connor Batty (11)
Magdalen College School

Shadows

I follow you everywhere,
But you won't hear a sound,
Not even a breath,
Or footsteps on the ground.

I appear only in daytime,
When the sun's shining bright,
As I cannot be seen,
In the darkness of night.

I wish I could speak,
Or just do my own thing,
Instead of copying you all day,
It's kind of boring!

Sophie Skinner (12)
Magdalen College School

N5N1

It was tragic and deadly,
It was called 'Bird flu',
Birds brought it in,
Scientists worried because it was new.

People they panicked,
People they died,
Nobody could stop it,
Although they tried.

Everyone was losing relatives,
Next it could be them,
No one could predict the future,
This caused major mayhem.

Time went by,
It got worse and worse,
It annihilated innocent people,
They all left in a hearse.

It went on a rampage,
Killed everything in sight,
The human race was ending,
Because of the bird in flight.

It hadn't yet reached,
The whole of the Earth,
Is this only the beginning,
Of the disease at birth?

Will anyone live to tell the tale?
That's what we wonder,
The flu had no mercy,
It just came to plunder.

Josie Isted (12)
Magdalen College School

I Have A Dream

Dream with light,
The children in Africa won't sleep tonight,
All alone in the cold night they will cry,
Looking up into a starlit sky,
Knowing soon they too will die,
So all they can do is cry.

When the sun rises up, so does the heat,
They wander around knowing there is nothing to eat,
Wandering around and around,
Dusty feet kicking the ground,
Walking around looking for water,
Parents know they have just lost their daughter.

Down goes the sun,
With the shot of a gun,
Look up to the sky,
Keep on wishing you could fly,
Never ever wanting to go,
So don't let time go slow.

Matthew Neal (12)
Magdalen College School

Silence

Silence,
Can roar like a hundred lions,
When not expected.
Silence,
Can float away like a feather,
When the time is right.
Silence,
Can truly taunt you,
When not wanted.
Silence,
Can explain it all,
When just needed.

Silence,
Can put words in your mouth,
Or take them away,
Can release all your worries,
Or cram them back in,
Can make you finally realise,
Or confuse you further.

But sometimes,
We forget about silence.
So just take a moment,
Right now . . .

There it goes again.

Ellen Edmondson (12)
Magdalen College School

Through The Eyes Of A Cloud

Drifting through the sky,
Floating like a boat,
I see all the birds fly
In their feather coats.

Over cities, towns and more,
Over farms as well,
Fields like a wonderful, carpeted floor,
A beautiful land I can tell.

Me and all my fluffy friends,
Gliding here and there,
I hope this ride will never end,
Dancing through the air.

I feel myself getting large
And rain begins to fall,
I feed the plants in people's yards,
So they grow quite tall.

When I'm finished, the night has come
And the moon and stars come out,
This day I've had has been great fun,
I loved it without a doubt.

Rebecca Berry (12)
Magdalen College School

Differences

They're rich, I'm poor,
Every year they get more.
I love the look of their food,
It makes me want to intrude.
They're dry, I'm wet,
There's no surprise we haven't met.
We're so different in every way,
Maybe I'll be like them one day.

Abigail Ogle (12)
Magdalen College School

Beauty To The Blind

I cannot see but I can hear
A fresh spring day when dawn is near
The flowers blooming in the ray
Of the sun before the day
The chirrup of birds, the swoosh of planes
Springtime is now here again
I may be blind but I can see
The beauty that's surrounding me
I cannot see but I can hear
A fresh spring day when dawn is near.

Charlotte Blackwell (11)
Magdalen College School

Out Of The Window

I was looking out the window with nothing to do,
There was a man walking down the road, slowly stumbling,
He seemed to be having trouble, fingers fumbling,
There must be something I could do.

I was still watching three minutes later,
There was that man crossing the road, walking steadily,
He did need help so I went, creeping cautiously,
There and then I helped.

I helped him carefully across the road,
There he stood staring into thin air, spookily scary,
He thanked me like I'd always known him, graciously grateful,
I heard him say as I walked away,
'I am blind.'

Emily Collinson (11)
Magdalen College School

The Christmas Turkey

Christmas is fun, Christmas is cool,
Christmas Day is enjoyed by all,
Except for the turkey, for him there is fear,
For him it's the worst day of the year!

He's the unlucky one, what a poor chum,
He has to have stuffing shoved up his bum,
Then he's put in the oven with one thought in his head,
Why, oh why can't they have chicken instead?

The other turkeys cry, whine and moan,
As their mate is eaten right down to the bone,
All they can do is cry all day,
As you eat, dance, laugh and play.

The turkeys are all upset about poor Bob,
Long after you've shovelled him into your gob,
They're planning revenge, let me give you a clue,
The person they're planning revenge on is you!

Chloe Hope (11)
Magdalen College School

I Went To School

I went to school today,
Like I do every day.
Nothing interesting happened in class,
I wish it will be over fast!

But on Monday it was fun,
None of it made me glum,
Because it was Sports Day today,
On a nice day in May.

Now on Tuesday it was scary,
A new girl came called Mary.
She bullied me and hit me,
But she made sure no one would see.

So on Wednesday it was boring,
In class I was yawning.
Finally, when school was over,
I got into my dad's red Rover.

Next, on Thursday I got detention,
I was fighting, who with I will not mention.
When I told my mum she was sad,
When I told my dad he was mad!

Finally, on Friday, last day to go,
Time seemed to go so slow.
I watched the clock, 3, 2, 1,
Yes, school work is done!

Hayley Duncan (12)
Magdalen College School

The Strawberry Poem

There I am standing on the ground,
Hiding under a leaf, hoping not to be found.
There she is, like a big baboon,
She has all my friends, they'll be in cream soon.

I am safe here in my keep,
I keep a watchful eye out in every peep.
I'm a strawberry, as lonely as can be,
I wish I was up there in that lovely tree.

She would never look there,
Not even if she were a bear.
When I awake the very next morning,
There I am sleepy and yawning.

They're my friends, they're not in cream,
This silly mistake must have all been a dream!

Shaun Eaton (12)
Magdalen College School

Fairground Senses

As I walk through the snow, 5 senses to go

I hear the excited sound of children laughing,
The gruesome groans from drunks barfing,
Piercing shrieks from one of the scary rides
And carnies shouting at my sides.

As I walk through the snow, 4 senses to go

I smell the damp on carnies' clothes
And the cotton candy by my nose,
I smell the toilets and the rusty drains,
The jam doughnuts, but they're only plain.

As I walk through the snow, 3 senses to go

I can feel the cold rushing through me
And notes vibrating as guitarists find their key,
The damp from the uncomfortable seat
And the ground moving from under my feet.

As I walk through the snow, 2 senses to go

I can see the blinding strobe lighting
And drunks from the pub viciously fighting,
I see people cold in the face
And others digging into their plaice

As I walk through the snow, 1 sense to go

The dust in my mouth that tastes sandy,
Which is taken away by the sweet cotton candy.
The fizz from soda, trickling down my throat
And the corn dogs that have a chocolatey coat.

As I walk through the snow, there is nowhere left to go.

Tom Halder (12)
Roade School

Five Senses

I can hear the fireworks crackling in the sky
I can see the children walking happily by
I can taste the candyfloss melting on my tongue
I can feel the shock of the bells being rung
I can smell the smoke wafting through the air

There are lots of things happening today at the fair

I can hear the music from the fair rides
I can see the children playing, they are trying to hide
I can taste the soft, sugary doughnut pressing against my lips
I can feel the wind blowing past my fingertips
I can smell fish and chips, but I don't really care

There are lots of things happening today at the fair.

Charlotte Barrie (11)
Roade School

At The Fair

Seeing flashing lights all around
I can feel my best friend's arm linked to mine
Sweet smell of candyfloss fills the air
The sound of children having fun rumbles in my head
Warm hot chocolate sizzles on my tongue
Strolling through the fair
In the autumn air.

Children sitting open-mouthed as they whizz round on rides
The softness of my gloves makes my hands warm and cosy
The smell of sizzling hot dogs goes through the air
Children demanding money from tired and stressed parents
The sugary taste of candyfloss sits on my tongue
Strolling through the fair
In the autumn air.

I see children clutching teddies they've won
The cold bites viciously at my red face
As I go past the toilets, the smell makes me feel sick
The sound of stall owners shouting vibrates through my head
I can taste the horrible smoke from the pub as it wafts through
                                                          the fair

Strolling through the fair
In the autumn air.

Fireworks sparkle in front of my eyes
The cold metal of the roller coaster freezes up my back
The smell of petrol fills the car park
The deafening screams of children in my cold head
The cold fizz of cola bubbles on my tongue
Strolling through the fair
In the autumn air.

Lucy Miller (11)
Roade School

Homework, Oh Homework!

Homework, oh homework,
I hate you, you stink!

I wish I could wash you
Away in the sink.

I wish the wind would blow you away
For me to do another day.

I wish I could jump on your creases
And rip you to pieces.

Homework, oh homework,
I hate you, you stink!

Georgina Baker & Sydney Marston (12)
Roade School

Friend

I've got a friend called Dale
He sometimes goes pale

He's a good mate
He has a friend called Kate

He's a goalkeeping star
Better than Van der Sar

He can stop all goals
Even from Paul Scholes

We have had our ups and downs
We will pull frowns

We play for the same football team
Roade Rangers is our team

He is my best friend
From now to the end.

Jamie Wilby (13)
Roade School

Life

Cold, terror,
I felt that night,
No one knew of my fright,
My blood was as cold as ice.

Shiver, damp,
This is my life,
I have no chance to love a wife,
Off I go, moved on, now twice.

Parched, starvation,
No food anywhere in sight,
All I do is pray for light,
Watch your toes, those mice, they bite.

Life
The world's at my feet,
Will I live another day, walking along the beat,
Or will I kill myself.

Slitting my wrists
Is the only solution
To a problem beyond control,
Down I fall, one dosser less.

No one cares, just clean up the mess,
Now I'm buried down, down deep,
No one mopes, no one weeps,
'Cause my life is over.

Samantha Green (13)
Roade School

Homeless

I walked down the cold street
I could feel blisters on my feet
Rain dropped on my head
I felt as though I was dead
My stomach ached with hunger
I could hear the thunder
Nobody cares about me
Everyone just leaves me be
I ask for some spare cash
And off you all run in a dash
I walked down the cold street
I could feel blisters on my feet.

Josh Savage (12)
Roade School

Tourette's

Looking through his eyes, I see fear and confusion.
He feels darkness, he smells twitches, but doesn't know why.
He crawls, falls and cries.
He hears voices, shouts. He shakes, shudders,
Loneliness crawls upon him, he's fed up but it won't go away.
Voices, screams, shouts.
He tries to wake up, but it will never vanish,
He knows it but can't face the thoughts,
So he curls up and remembers his old life.
He will never be the same,
But only he knows why.

Mette Smith (13)
Roade School

The Meaning Of Life

Life,
Is it whole?
Maybe a knife,
Or my soul.

But I shall never know.
I am homeless
And on the street,
So . . .
The world at my feet.

I have lost my best mate
And nothing is the same.
Now it will be my fate.
What is my name?

No,
Let me think!
I know,
It's Link.

Sean Tidder (13)
Roade School

My World

My world is like Heaven,
We travel around and have trips to Devon.
The sun shines brighter than ever,
Look, there's my friend, Heather.
Chocolate cherries hang on the tree,
Charlotte and me,
Have to have our tea.
The moon shines in the night,
Alice gave me a very big fright.
Now the day is done,
Me and my mum,
Will have fun,
Tomorrow!

Abigail Breeds (11)
The Rushden Community College

My World

In my world everyone's nice,
In my world there are no wars,
In my world no one dies,
In my world there are no bullies.

In my world no animals are killed,
In my world families are together,
In my world everyone is treated the same,
In my world there's no pollution.

In my world everyone's happy,
In my world there are no tramps,
In my world there's no vandalism,
In my world everyone's different.

In my world everything's pretty,
In my world nothing's damaged,
In my world you can live anywhere,
In my world there are no taxes.

In my world there's no racism,
In my world everyone's got water,
In my world you have fun,
In my world you don't work.

In my world you have the freedom to talk,
In my world everyone's safe,
    My world is happy.

Daniel Piper (11)
The Rushden Community College

A View From A Pen

I'm stuck in this lonely pencil case,
With pencils and rulers alike,
I'm taken out six times a week,
But at weekends I'm left alone.

It's dark in the lonely pencil case,
I wish I had some friends,
But all the pencils gang up on me
And the rulers are just as bad.

I wish I had an exciting life,
Like people and other things,
But that is never going to happen,
So I might as well live with it.

Amy Northwood (11)
The Rushden Community College

My World

My world is huge
My world is fun
We play, play, play
My world, you never get bored
My world is cool
My world, there are no rules
My world, there are beaches
You can feel the sand and smell the sea
My world, there's no school
Instead, we play and have lots of fun
My world is the best
Come and join in the fun!

Hannah Robinson (11)
The Rushden Community College

My World

My world to me is like the . . .
Sunshine, all bright and happy
No sadness
My world to me is like a . . .
Big ball of fun
It's bouncy
And funny
My world to me is like a . . .
Friendship circle
Full of my friends, Rachel, Rhia and Tisha
And my best mate, Abi
My world to me is like a . . .
Desert island
All quiet
All beautiful, let your memories drift
My world to me is like a . . .
Painting
All brushstrokes
Such delicate paint
My world to me is like a . . .
Space
So much to see
All pretty sights
But not much time to see it
That's what my world is to me.

Alice Savage (12)
The Rushden Community College

My Life As A Fish

My world is lonely,
My world is sad,
I swim in the ocean,
I swim in the sea,
I'm all on my own,
Just me and the water,
I wish I had a new friend,
Not just the seaweed,
I really hate it on my own,
I'm a lonely little fish,
I'm a blue and yellow fish,
I live amongst the seaweed,
It's just me and the sea,
All I do is swim, swim, swim,
I get tired from all that swimming,
At least I'm a free fish,
Unlike some who are trapped in a small, cold fish tank.

Emma Fett (12)
The Rushden Community College

My World

My world is different depending on the day,
If I'm at school or at home to play.
If I'm at school I don't have fun,
But if it's the weekend I have fun eating a bun.
When it's time for school again, I moan,
I get there and meet my friends, my moan is not shown.
School starts, I walk to class,
I'm not usually one of the last.
I go home at the bell,
I feel like a snail going into my shell.
I have one sister who is always in her room,
If I enter that room, I'm at doom.
The weekend arrives and I go shopping,
I hear my lemonade randomly popping.
Well, that's my world, full of fun, except for school,
The best part of my world is my mates, because they are cool.

Emily Williams (11)
The Rushden Community College

My World

Revving an engine on a KX65
At the swimming pool doing a dive
Playing football with a team
Having a sleep with a dream

I have a lot to eat for dinner
And watching others try to get thinner
I love my daily Brussels sprouts
It helps me very well to shout

And when I'm watching CBBC
I run around the room like a bee
My favourite show is definitely 'Arthur'
And it's funny and I laugh after

My world is the best
Better than the rest
I think it's really cool
And it's up to me, so you should.

Charlz Whitehouse (12)
The Rushden Community College

My World

A place full of life
With such wonders to see
A sweet-scented rose
Attracting a bee.
A beautiful sunset
Above the sea
A wonderful bird
Singing with glee.
Tall, rocky mountains
Standing so high
Twinkling stars
Like fire in the sky.
All different creatures
Whether big or small
Despite if they fly
Even if they crawl.
Lovely scenery
Inspiring sights
The round, yellow moon
Fills the sky with lights.
Everything peaceful
And full of charm
This is my world
My world is calm.

Rachel Martin (12)
The Rushden Community College

My World

In my world the sun always shines
In my world nobody works in mines
In my world there are no wars
In my world there are no closed doors
In my world people are nice
In my world there are no mice
In my world women rule
In my world men act the fool
In my world we are all friends
In my world the fun never ends
In my world the flowers grow
In my world the rivers flow
In my world the food is plenty
In my world the plates are never empty
In my world we think school is great
In my world there is no hate
In my world everyone's a star
In my world we never travel far
In my world we celebrate success
My world is never too far away
For me to go and have a play!

Emily Fensome (11)
The Rushden Community College

My World

Amazing creatures wander far,
Vehicles roam streets, lorries, vans, cars,
The echoing sound of a baby's cry,
In the clear blue sky, birds fly.
My world is full of happiness and love,
Like the symbol of a white, beautiful dove,
Trees sway in the fresh summer breeze,
The repeating sound of an ill person's sneeze.
My world is full of life and joy,
My world is full of wonderful things,
It gives us everything it has to give.

Rebekah Hobbs (12)
The Rushden Community College

My World

My world is fun
My world is cool
My world has no law
But no one's dead on the floor

My world has no schools
We make our own rules
My world is full
But we have only just begun.

My world is mine
My world is fine
My world is made by me
Do you agree?

Kaija McGregor (12)
The Rushden Community College

My World

My world is mad,
But in no way bad.
The people are daring,
But yet they are all caring.

My world can be polluted,
But yet we are all suited,
My world has no wars,
Just full of open doors.

My world is full of harmony,
Sweet music to one's ears.

No fights,
No wars,
More peace,
More cause.

Jodie Groves (12)
The Rushden Community College

Mobile Phone

Why?
Why?
Why do people talk into me
Without noticing I talk back to them?
I feel like a slave inside of myself.
I sit alone in his pocket,
I get dropped, but he doesn't care.
He will either throw me away or sell me off.
I will break but he doesn't care.
Older and older I get,
Then it happens, I don't work.
I don't have a life.

Thomas Alexander (11)
The Rushden Community College

My World

My world is like a holiday
My world is as hot as an oven
My world is purple and pink
And nobody has a stink on them
My world is full of hope
With all your friends to help
Kayleigh, Emma, Sammy and Sammy
My world has no teachers
Which makes me happy
My world has no one sad
Which is not so bad
My world has no schools
Which makes it sound so cool
Well, that's my world
The best world.

Alice Hicks (11)
The Rushden Community College

Dog Days

It's not so much the running as the pacing,
Back and forth before the door,
The scratching of pain, fleas that sting
With a humiliating smallness.

And what of dreams?
Running in one's sleep, small whimpers,
Tight leashes leading nowhere very far at all,
Circles, circles three times always,
Nose to the ground,
Holding still for that absent-minded pat,
Hopelessly affectionate despite sudden inclinations.
Run to the end of the yard and I may jump the fence.

Hollie Gordge (13)
The Rushden Community College

Poor Tara

I cannot speak
I am paralysed
The way I talk
Is through my eyes.

I'm in a bed
I can't eat food
I have to be fed
Through a tube.

I'm in the hospital
With no family here
It's all deserted
With no one near.

I try my best
To break a smile
But nothing happens
Not even for a while.

My name is Tara
I'm six years of age
I feel useless
Like a bird in a cage.

Lauren Tennant (13)
The Rushden Community College

Cars

I turn green, then I turn red
Oh, why can't I turn blue instead?
I see the drivers swear at me,
Oh, why can't they just leave me be?
I'm stuck here watching the world go by
And sometimes I just think and wonder why.
What if cars were never made?
I start to see my future fade.
What if lorries weren't whizzing along the road,
Hurrying past with their heavy load?
What if cars weren't thought of by some guy,
Then I would not be made, oh why?
But cars were made, it is true,
There are lots of cars, old and new
And now I see my future is bright,
Even though I am just a traffic light.

Evangeline Maddams (13)
The Rushden Community College

A Tree's Life

I stand in the park
Slowly growing old
In summer I am nice and warm
In winter I am bald and cold

Every day I see hundreds pass
As each year passes, I lose my green
Most people use me as shade
I have once even given shade to the Queen

I can almost touch the sky
Since I am so high
I stand out from the rest
A house could just reach my thigh

When the park closes
I become all alone
When it opens in the morning
I smell the scent of an ice cream cone.

Huy Ta (12)
The Rushden Community College

Shadow

I have no say in what I do,
Whatever you do, I must do too.

I mimic without a choice of my own,
When we go, I go to your home.

In the day I rise very tall,
By midday I am very small.

At night I come and go as you choose,
But all the time I'm hard to lose.

I lead the life that you do,
But I feel no emotions, unlike you.

Anna Jane (12)
The Rushden Community College

In The Tree

When I'm sitting in the tree I can see,
The birds flying, tweeting and squawking.
I can see the foxes playing, running and catching prey,
I can feel the breeze blowing and the damp air in my fur.
Then I see two things running and barking fiercely.
My heart beats faster and I start sweating.
I run, terrified. I have never run so fast from such terrifying monsters.
But at last, I am back at the top of a tree.

Holly Mather (13)
The Rushden Community College

Little Bird, Big World

I am a little bird,
A bluebird flying in the sky,
I have freedom,
I can do whatever I want,
When I flap my wings,
I feel the breeze on my feathers.

I am a little bird,
A bluebird flying in the sky,
When I pick up my twigs and twine
To build my nest for others to lay eggs,
I fly out to get food, then come back to have a sleep,
Then I will carry on tomorrow.

I am a little bird,
A bluebird flying in the sky,
Whenever I wake up, I set out to explore the big, wide world.
I have freedom, so I can do whatever I want, when I want,
When I'm tired, I go to sleep and say goodnight,
Goodnight.

Ben Varney (12)
The Rushden Community College

Crystal

Crystal is the name of my rabbit,
She only died the other day.
She did have a very big habit
And she absolutely loved to lay!

I woke up Friday morning,
I heard my mum say,
'Rebecca, your rabbit looks poorly,
We might have to see the vet,
But what would we have to pay?'

I waited and waited,
For the last two days,
She hung on and hung on,
Till she faded away.

Early Sunday morning,
I heard my dad downstairs,
It was very early so obviously he was yawning,
He ran up and said, 'Becca, she didn't make it.'

Rebecca Dix (13)
The Rushden Community College

A Day At School

I'd like to stay at home today
But if I do I know what they will say
Five days a week I go to school
My mum says it's the rule
Even when it's wet and cold
I have to do as I am told
Each morning I begin my walk
With my friend I laugh and talk.

Terry Vickery (12)
The Rushden Community College

Poverty

P oor and needy
O bviously not greedy
V igilant for food
E veryone could help
R ich, more than others
T o help, give generously
Y ou could help too.

Domonic Long (13)
The Rushden Community College

Morocco

M orning in Morocco is quite beautiful, if I say so myself
O ver the sea the sun glistens across the horizon
R ocks surround the beach, stopping sand blowing in your face
O ceans all around the island
C rispy, delicious foods along the buffet
C ute cat hiding in the bush with its kittens
O h, what a fantastic experience this has been,
                            I hope I can visit again.

Kelly Barnes (11)
The Rushden Community College

The Wind

The wind is howling loud and clear,
Speaking to everyone that is near,
Trying to be heard and seen,
No one listens,
No one hears.

The wind is getting very angry,
Hitting walls
And making calls.

Tornado, tornado,
Don't come to that,
I'm furious, I'm mad,
I'm breaking walls,
I'm taking lives.

Why isn't anybody listening to me?
All I want is to be heard and seen.

Now the wind is calm and quiet,
Everybody hears,
Everybody listens.

Emma Betterton (11)
The Rushden Community College

Cheetahs

Cheetahs are killers,
Cheetahs are a thriller.
Cheetahs look for prey,
Cheetahs go hooray.

Cheetahs are hiding,
Cheetahs go finding.
Cheetahs are grinding,
Cheetahs are sliding.

Cheetahs are hunted,
Cheetahs' claws are blunted.
Cheetahs deserve a pat on the back,
Cheetahs' spots are black.

Cheetahs are so serious
Cheetahs are so delirious.
Cheetahs hide in flowers,
Cheetahs run 60 miles an hour.

Jonathan Jones (12)
The Rushden Community College

Elephants

Man is a hunter,
Man is a killer,
He hunts for our tusks,
We run for our lives, but they still can't catch us,
Someone please help us.

When the sun goes down,
The men go home,
The nightmare is over,
But in the morning,
It will start again,
Someone please help us.

We wake up,
No man in sight,
We are free,
Free from man,
Free from the nightmare,
We are saved.

Bang! We hear a gun,
The men are back,
The nightmare is back,
We are not free,
Someone please help us.

Kelsey MacGowan (11)
The Rushden Community College

If I Were A Cat

If I were a cat I could scratch and purr,
If I were a cat I would be stroked and adored,
If I were a cat I would never be bored,
If I were a cat I'd have a long tail,
If I were a cat I'd be female!

Gemma King (11)
The Rushden Community College

The Lotus

T racking engine
H igh horse power
E xpensive joy

L ush-looking bonnet
O verheated engine from nitrous
T ime stopper
U ndertaker king
S peed demon.

Arron Scroxton (12)
The Rushden Community College

My Cat

My cat
My cat is such a gentle soul
Although she's small, it's true
She brings the fish in her mouth
She brings the ocean too.

Shannon O'Dell (11)
The Rushden Community College

Dr Pepper

D rink and feel the taste
R eally nice

P riceless
E verlasting
P robably the best drink ever made
P recious
E xciting
R evs you up!

Jordan Jupp (11)
The Rushden Community College

Fame

I made a funny game
That had a lot of fame
It included a little dame
With a mind full of fame

I made a funny game
That gave you a lot of fame
This made people give up their name
To play this fun, wicked game

I made a funny game
That did everything the same
But when they played the game
They wanted more fame

I made a funny game
And this boy called Wayne
Wanted to play another game
And I said to him, there is no game like fame.

Traynie Atkins (12)
The Rushden Community College

Pollution

P olluting all the streets
O ver the floor and field
L oads of wrappers sparkling in the light
L ots of crisp packets in the night
U sually you all do it even if you don't admit it
T o all the animals it is cruel
I have seen people throw things on the floor
O h, my gosh, what a mess
N o one should do it anymore.

Leah Cudone (12)
The Rushden Community College

Dreams

I once had a dream,
That I could fly,
I flew across the town
And went very high,
Then all of a sudden, I started to shake,
I fell down and started to wake.

Rya Alice Willis-Jones (11)
The Rushden Community College

Football

F ootball is cool
O ut in the rain playing our socks off
O ut in the sun, still playing our socks off
T ime out! Half-time
B oot the ball in the back of the net
A ll of us cheering and celebrating
L et us claim our prizes and they are medals
L et us be off now, we have our prizes, so goodbye for now.

Tyler Stratford (11)
The Rushden Community College

Dolphins

D olphins have no say in life
O nly if they could shout, 'I'm down here, by the way'
L eave us pure
P lease save the Earth and be sure, by
H elping us to recycle and not pollute
I n the world we live today
N obody seems to care, so everybody help the animals and dolphins
S o please don't pollute the world!

Paris Wills (12)
The Rushden Community College

The Prey

I'm always stalked
Never am I allowed
Rest.

Enemy in front
Enemy behind
Enemy everywhere.

Running, fleeing
For our lives
We are never safe.

Has it gone?
Has it not?
I don't know.

We are dead
I am dead
We all fear the tiger.

I'm always stalked
Never am I allowed
Rest!

Adam Monger (11)
The Rushden Community College

Through The Dinosaur's Eyes

Through a dinosaur's eyes
The eyes that don't lie,
He sees many dangers of furious monsters,
The monsters come,
His eyes light in game
And runs down a lane,
Lost his game
And darkness comes
And a new days begins.

He opens his eyes,
He doesn't cry,
He lies down in fright,
Of a knight,
Of their monsters in their might.

He dies lying,
Crying,
Crying for help.

But then it goes dark,
As dark as a black heart,
He's gone away,
With his eyes open.

Jordon Brown (11)
The Rushden Community College

Bullying

B eating you up
U nless you can run
L ivers smashed
L ives taken
Y ou are going to die
I gnoring you when you speak
N ever mind you're hurt
G oing to get you again.

Kieran Foster (11)
The Rushden Community College

Still Poem

I am very smart, although I cannot hear, speak, see or smell,
I may not have a brain,
But I do have a lot of information in me,
It is mostly spellings and word meanings,
People use me a lot,
I'm not hard to spot,
I am very sorry now, but I must go.

Alex Honeywood (11)
The Rushden Community College

I'm A Bus

I'm a bus
I make no fuss
I pick up people
All day long
In the pouring rain
And the boiling sun.

Jordan Thornton (12)
The Rushden Community College

Day And Night

Day and night, I sit in brown,
Day and night, I feel like a clown,
Day and night, I sit in New York,
Day and night, I was hurt and had no food before,
Day and night, I watch people go past,
Day and night, I wish someone would pick me up,
Day and night, on my own, lonely as can be,
Day and night, I can see,
Today I'm picked up by Balone,
Day and night, I have a home.

Chantelle Wornast-Humphreys (11)
The Rushden Community College

Cloud

I am high,
I cannot fly,
I am white,
I cannot die,
I am fat,
But not when I cry,
People think it is rain,
I am so high,
So very, very high,
But sometimes I'm scared of heights,
I am in the sky,
What am I?

Steven Edwards (12)
The Rushden Community College

The Tree

I stand here all alone
While those kids whine and moan
I love the sun
It's my mum
My roots are strong
And I live long
I make no fuss
Not like a bus
I am a tree,
Yep, that's me.

Brent Wills (11)
The Rushden Community College

The Tree That Couldn't See

There is a tree
That couldn't see
But kids pee
On me
I frown and grin
When the kids go in
I try to walk
And wind helps me
I get out the ground
Whining loud
But no one knows
I'm falling down
Here I am
No one around
Whining loud
I'm dying
But I was lying
I could see
But not for me
I'm closing my eyes
About to die
But woe is me
I'm dead, just for me
But will I live
To tell the tale?
Truth says no
'Cause I have to go
But I have to say
Another line
I smell of lime.

Peter Sanders (12)
The Rushden Community College

The Chair

I cannot see
I may not have ears
But I hear them speak

I feel the pain
I don't say a word
But here I am, with many others

I'm used every day
I only relax twice a day, weekends and nights
It smells sometimes, very bad

At a table all the time
Getting hurt all the time
Help me, before I break.

Luke Davis (12)
The Rushden Community College

I'm A Load Of Dangly Hair Looking For A Mate . . .

I'm a load of hair braided, wavy or straight,
I hang around all day, just looking for a mate,
Do you use Garnier, Timotei or any?
I'm living just like any day, with not even a penny.

I'm a load of hair, sobbing around all day,
Please come and play with me, or just take me away,
I have to visit the hairdresser to cut off those split ends,
Please come and play with me, I'm looking for some friends.

I'm a load of hair dyed, normal or short,
Please come and help me live the life I bought,
You can tie me up or just leave me down,
I'm a load of hair, sometimes with a smile, or a frown.

I'm a load of hair dangling, dangling hair,
Please look after me with tender, loving care,
Will you either brush or comb me too,
I'm a load of boring hair, with not even one thing to do.

I'm a load of hair, braided, wavy or straight,
I hang around all day, just looking for a mate,
Do you use Garnier, Timotei or any?
I'm living the life you bought me, with not even a penny.

Charlotte Andrews (12)
The Rushden Community College

The Puppy

I stand here all alone
Gnawing a bone
I lay down on my bed
All alone
People look at me
Walk straight past
I want a home, fast
Before time does pass
Please someone take me home
Bring a lovely, juicy bone
Take me to your house
Let me have a squeaky mouse.

Hannah Samanon (11)
The Rushden Community College

Statue In The Park

I am a statue
I live in a park
I've been in the park a long time
And I'm not very happy to be me
People look at me and walk away

I am a statue
I live in a shed
All scared and unhappy.

Joana Read (11)
The Rushden Community College

I'm A Tree

Hello, I'm a tree,
That cannot see,
But I can frown,
I wear a crown,
I smile so big,
I have a twig,
So, so, long
My pong is really strong,
Kids climb on me,
I need to see,
I hear the wind,
I like tinned,
Veg, I do,
But I need a poo.

Jamie-Leigh Smith (12)
The Rushden Community College

The Fly

I am a fly
I like to lie
My favourite food is raspberry pie
I'm mischievous and sly
I creep and fly.

Harry Stevenson (11)
The Rushden Community College

PlayStation 2 - Games Console

Yippee! Someone comes to play,
I've been waiting for them all day!
I welcome them in
And say hello,
But instead, they decide to play the cello!

I play new games,
Almost every day,
Someone shouts and screams,
But I don't know why,
Don't ask me, but they're about to cry!

Au revoir, I've got to go,
Because I think it's about to snow,
One last thing I'd like to say,
Who am I?

Hayden Pott (11)
The Rushden Community College

Hadrian's Wall

They come, they go,
Day and night,
Men and women,
I watch without comment,
For I cannot speak,
I have no mouth,
Yet I am not weak,
In Roman times I stood,
Tall against the Barbarians,
Waiting to attack me, the wall,
Between them and victory,
Nowadays people come,
To visit and look at me,
I watch the tourists,
Without comment,
For I cannot speak.

Adam Lonergan (12)
The Rushden Community College

Lined Paper

I like to stay with my friends, in a wad,
I like my place,
It's warm, dark and absolutely fantastic,
But then, I'm taken away from my friends,
I'm left alone with some alien staring at me,
It brings out a pen and starts scribbling,
Argh! It hurts!

They carry on hurting me,
Yay, now they've stopped,
But I'm left lying alone,
In the end, I am screwed up
And just thrown in the bin.

Sarah Hanson (12)
The Rushden Community College

Turning Back Time

If I could turn back time,
I would stop the Arctic from melting,
The polar bears would worship me,
If I saved their homes,
The rising water from the melting snow,
Would save us all from a watery grave,
The world would be a wonderful place,
That everyone would enjoy.

If I could turn back time,
I would stop World Wars I and II from happening,
The kings would be so grateful,
They would dub me Peacemaker,
I would bring peace to Iraq,
The children would think I was a lord,
The world would be a peaceful place,
For us all.

If I could turn back time,
I would create a medicine for the Black Death,
It would stop children young and old from dying,
They would make me a doctor,
I would build a hospital,
I would stop murders from happening,
People would live longer,
They would not be able to find words to say thank you
The people would have a happy life
No more horrible death is how I end this.

Rebecca Key (12)
The Rushden Community College

This World

Our world is suffering on our behalf
Draining away our resources
Sucking the life out of our planet
Beckoning Nature's forces.

Polluting the world without a thought
Making our lives Hell
Thinking could make a difference
These words I must tell

Our planet is fading away
Drifting into shadow
The time has nearly come
The thread we hang on to is narrow

I see beyond the darkness
I see past the illusion
My mind is cloudy with thought
Because of this confusion

People think, but do nothing
The time is drawing near
Before we know it, our lives will change
And we will all be full of fear.

Samuel Perry (12)
The Rushden Community College

The Meaning Of Life

The meaning of life might be to eat pie
The meaning of life might be to die
The meaning of life might be to cry
The meaning of life might be to fry
The meaning of life might be to fly

The meaning of life might be to worship kings
The meaning of life might be to have rings
The meaning of life might be to take whatever life brings
The meaning of life might be to use swings
The meaning of life might be to have things

The meaning of life might be to have snow
The meaning of life might be for rivers to flow
The meaning of life might be for things to be low
The meaning of life, we don't know.

Travis Price (13)
The Rushden Community College

The Meaning Of Life

Have you ever wondered about the meaning of life?
Think about the newborn babies and the chirping birds,
Growing up throughout all the years,
Think about the meaning of life, just listen to my words,
We are all different in our own ways, mouth, nose and ears.

Have you ever wondered about the meaning of life?
What do you think? It's your opinion that matters,
All over the world there are different races,
The weather changing daily, listen to the rain as it patters,
Doesn't matter about the colour of your skin, or about your faces,
That's the meaning of life.

Brittany Scott (12)
The Rushden Community College

Secret Confessions

I need to make a confession
Our love led to obsession
Broken hearts triggered my depression
Then more and more aggression

It's hard for me to say
Because you treated me that way
It's so hard to trust when people betray
But I think of you each day

Where did we go wrong?
It worked well for so long
Surely it's time that I moved on?
But it's hard now that you have gone

Laying here every single night
It's no longer a fight
A change in my life has to be right
Thinking of the future is now my sight.

Katie Lawman (12)
The Rushden Community College

Lucky Kick

I have watched a lot
Of football in my life
And have dreamed of playing
Some day

I saw the football
On TV last night
Penalty kicks
All the way

After the game
I went to bed
And dreams of football
Ran through my head

I was picked to kick
So I kicked that ball
As hard as I could
And it flew, just like a jet

I really kicked hard
It was a ball on fire
That burnt its way
Into the back of the net!

Matthew White (12)
The Rushden Community College

My World Belongs To Me

I cross my legs, then close my eyes
And try to understand,
That there are lots of people in the world
And I am one of them.

Slowly the noise and light disappears
And as I'm left on my own again,
I hear whispers in the bushes
And a bird singing in the tree.

These noises around me make me calm
And also very peaceful,
So that I finally understand,
That as I control this world,
It therefore, belongs to *me!*

Jodi Wills (11)
The Rushden Community College

Statue Of Liberty

I stand tall in the morning
Watching over New York,
The sunlight strikes my back
But I can't look behind,
I'm stuck to this beautiful spot
And I'm really easy to find.

The tourists come to see me
While the people of New York
Begin their busy day,
I am the main attraction,
Unique in every way.

They climb up many steps,
Right up to my crown,
Just to see my wonderful view,
I'm very busy most days
And usually there's a queue.

My hands hold a book of knowledge
And a torch of wisdom
This is why I am
The Statue of Liberty.

Ben Warren (13)
The Rushden Community College

Fantasy Forest

Walking through the forest;
Looking through these eyes;
Determined to be able to fear no living lives;
The wind blows through my hair;
The melody is flowing;
One wish of a fantasy;
But time is slowly choking;
Our mind power is so strong;
Can take us around this world;
Thoughts that we believe are wrong;
Left alone to cry, a tender child;
As I walk through the forest;
I see these are not my eyes;
Forever I will listen to these dying lives;
This is not a fantasy.

Jade Scott (12)
The Rushden Community College

The First Thing I Saw:

Memory stick, memory stick,
How convenient you are to me.
All my files, right by my side;
You make me so happy.

You look after my games,
Illegal programs and hacks.
What would I do without you?
Probably borrow Jack's.

Your unbelievable features:
High-speed USB,
Only the ultimate for you, my friend,
In ways of connectivity.

Your unmatchable convenience,
There, whenever I need.
Unlike any friend I've had,
But with you, I cannot breed.

My thanks goes to Play.com,
For producing this great device,
I could not be more grateful,
For your fantastically low-cut price.

I think I should stop writing now,
I'm running out of ideas,
Oh, wait, I have but one more left,
As your little red light appears.

I shall give this poem to you, my friend,
To whom I will be true,
Translate it into your language,
That is FAT32!

Hughie Wilmshurst (16)
The Rushden Community College

Football

F ootball is so great
O ut on the field on a sunny day
O ff the field, 1-0 up at half-time
T errific half for all the lads
B ands play as we come off the pitch
A s they applaud, the band bows
L et's go out again and show them who's boss
L ads, come on!

Aaron Swingler (12)
The Rushden Community College

A Dog's Life

My dreams hover above my head
My elegance stuns my species
A dog is what I am, but god I am inside,
I feel the gentle breeze and freeze
Endless chains on the street, as I start to grow pains.

Big dogs, small dogs, we're all the same
Some of us live on the street
While others live in a house.

Daniel Todd (11)
The Rushden Community College

Friendships

Friendships can change, like the passing of the tide,
But they are still strong,
As time passes by.
I thought those laughs would be forever.
But then came the day,
I knew they would stop.
I promised to you I wouldn't leave without a fight
And a fight I put up . . .
To no success.
I know we swore - best friends forever,
Now it's all changed,
Though I refuse to let go.
No matter what, I won't forget,
Those laughs, cries,
Good times and bad.
That part has passed in my childhood life,
I've learned to live,
With the way things are.
I told you my secrets and you told me yours,
But I have good friends,
That I now can trust.
They'll never replace my thoughts of you,
I'm torn apart,
Between two separate worlds.

Emily Dimmock (13)
The Rushden Community College

Sad Life Of Penguins

We penguins have no food
'Cause you children pollute
No one cares about us now
People used to say, *Aww!* Look at them penguins'
And now they say, *'Eww!* They're stinky!'
All because your children leave pollution in my area
And now all my friends are dying.

Chloe Gallon (12)
The Rushden Community College

Goodbye

I looked into his eyes,
As I left him behind,
There are tears running down my face,
I don't want to be in this horrible place,
Why did this happen to me?
Why let him die?
He's up in Heaven now,
Right up in the sky,
I went to his funeral,
All dressed in black,
No matter how much I try,
I can never get you back,
You're being lowered into the ground,
I can feel my heart pound,
I wish this didn't happen,
But it will never change,
I will always be with you,
No matter where you are,
A grandad, that's what you are to me
And that's the way it will always be.

Stacey Joyce (13)
The Rushden Community College

Guns

If everyone had a gun,
They would shoot everyone,
Shops would be on fire,
World Wars would break out,
There would be World War III, IV and V,
Loads of people would die.

Charlie Clayton (12)
The Rushden Community College

My Broken Heart

If I could turn back time
You would still be mine
I think about you all the while
You always make me laugh and smile
Pressure pushing down on me
I wish that you didn't leave.

I look up at the stars and cry
And time is still flying by
I wanted to give you my heart
You took it and tore it apart
Why do I still love you?
I don't even want to
I thought that we would last
We could forget about our past.

I want you to hold me tight
And kiss me all through the night.

Natasha Brown (12)
The Rushden Community College

Just Been Born

I've just been born,
Everything's a blur,
I feel very helpless,
I keep hearing noises,
What could they be?
I feel quite cold,
I need a hug,
Who will hug me?
Will they be nice?
What is my name?
Who are my family?
I really don't know,
I feel quite helpless,
Someone help me,
I'm only a baby,
I see things moving,
Things kissing my head,
Am I safe here?
I'm only a baby,
I feel hands wrapping round me,
I suddenly get lifted up,
Are you my family? Am I safe?
I feel more things kissing my head,
How will I know I'm safe in your arms?
I feel warm and loved,
This is my family,
I feel safe now,
Safe in your arms.

Jessica Davey (12)
The Rushden Community College

WWII Baby

The cold wind rushed over my tender skin,
I cried and screamed as the cold hit me,
A rough towel rubbed my skin,
It itched all over.
A short, sharp pain ran through my body,
As the umbilical cord was cut,
I was alone,
As one,
No food going into my bloodstream.
A huge siren screamed
And screams and cries filled the ward,
The nurse took me in her smooth, soft hands,
I cried as my mother seemed so far away from me.
'Your father will be here soon to save us,' said the nurse.
What did she mean?
Where is he?
Why is he not here?
A huge shelter I was put in,
I was now alone,
No one in here,
Just me.
A huge bang,
Silence there was,
A man screamed,
Another bang,
Bombs were exploding,
The roof shook,
The siren went off.

The only *survivor!*
Alone in the Blitz,
I was scared.

Aaron Sinclair (13)
The Rushden Community College

Why Do People Bully Me?

Why do people bully me?
Through this poem you will see
I get bullied cos of my bodyweight
Although I sometimes have to retaliate.
My family is placed everywhere
When I go there people stare,
I want to change what I do
The person I am, sank to the bottom of my shoe
I will let the person out someday
I will just stay there and pray.

Don't get bullied, stick up for yourself.

Katie Kirkup (13)
The Rushden Community College

What Hurts The Most?

What hurts the most is a question
That has to be answered
Bullying is bad
Hurtful comments are sad
And the people getting bullied need help
Just like me
I am getting bullied
My heart feels like it's polluted
My voice is in a distant forest
Where the wolves will rip it apart
All the days I have had
They have been mad
Physical fighting takes place
So it gives me a funny taste
I wish I could tell them to go away
But they know they can pick on me all day
So here is my time to say goodbye
To all those good days in my life
Because I'm gonna get kicked and taken the mick
So now you know what hurts the most.

Justine Abbott (13)
The Rushden Community College

Bird Flu

I am a chicken
Bird flu is on the loose
And the farmer has started kicking
He's getting us outside, I say goodbye to Mr Goose

We're going to be gassed
Or shot
As some have in the past
I don't know a lot

There's nothing wrong with us
Bird flu is a load of nothing
I want the escape bus
I want a big muffin

Farmer's got his gun
Soon it will be done
I'm gonna be shot
I'll be nothing but a dot

We are all in a line
The rest think we'll be fine
We're shot, one by one
I'm next, it's not a lot of fun
Bang!
Bang!
That's the end of me and my gang.

Sam Loak (12)
The Rushden Community College

A Horse's Life

It's a cold, windy day,
I am tied up for sale,
Three days have gone by,
A girl comes along and stares in my eyes,
She knows I am the one for her,
The money I see comes out of her mother's pocket,
'I will take this one,' I hear,
Clip-clop, I go happily as ever,
I go into my room, the stable and sleep,
The next day I have something touch my back,
What is it?
A saddle!
The girl is going to ride me . . .
Off the track and onto the grass I go,
Running as free as a wild horse,
Now we have to go home,
One of my dreams has come true!

Lauren Nicole Sulphur (12)
The Rushden Community College

If I Could Turn Back Time

If I could turn back time,
I would change nothing,
The world went by,
The birds sang,
Everything was as meant to be,
I made my mistakes,
I did my wrongs,
But at least I loved,
I would not change the bad things,
They happened for a reason,
We had no control over it
And that's what destiny is.

Luke Daniel Howe (11)
The Rushden Community College

Disneyland

Today I'm going to Disneyland, what will I be?
Today I'm going to play with Pooh sticks
Today I'm going to be Pooh Bear.

Yesterday, I was in a little tree house
Yesterday, I played with Pooh and Tigger
Yesterday, I was Piglet.

Tomorrow, what park shall I be in?
Tomorrow, I'm going to bounce all day,
Tomorrow, I'm going to be Tigger!

Leanne Denton (12)
The Rushden Community College

My World

My world is a world of colour and cheer,
Where no bullies laugh or sneer,
Tropical birds swoop and soar,
Where there is peace and without war,
My world is calm, free and wild
And the weather it hot, but not too mild.

Christopher Warren (12)
The Rushden Community College

True Love

His big blue eyes glistened in the sun,
His hair blowing in the breeze,
He glanced at me,
I glanced at him,
I couldn't breathe,
I froze in amazement,
How could this be?
I walked over to him,
Then we shared true love's first kiss.

Our love blossomed between us both,
Each day we shared together,
I never thought this day would come,
For me to say,
I've found the one,
Now that day has come
I know it's worth the wait,
How could I have been so dumb,
To push my feelings aside?
I always knew I loved him,
He really is the one for me.

Paige Kilsby (12)
The Rushden Community College

What Do You See?

What do you see when you look at me?
Just an old woman, nothing to say,
Is that why you laugh at me every day?
Poking and prodding me like I don't care
And there's nothing I can do, but sit and stare,
You shove food down me, like an animal at the zoo,
Because you know there's nothing I can do.

What do you see when you look at me?
Do you think I'm mad?
A distant memory of the life I once had,
That's why you yell if I don't get it right
And leave a bruise if I wake in the night,
You stare at me like I don't have a clue,
But I do.

What do you see when you look at me?
A woman with no voice?
A woman with no choice?
You yell so loud in my ear,
It's all I can hear,
My family live so far away
And they do not care anyway.

But there is no one to speak for me
And nothing will change . . .

Ever.

Cassie Reed (13)
The Rushden Community College

Differences

Life is Heaven for me
Life is Hell for me
I have a beautiful home
I live on the streets
I am waited on hand and foot
I have to beg
I have all the friends in the world
I have no friends
I have people to help me if I'm down
I'm constantly in pain
My dad is a billionaire
My dad is fighting
My mum is a duchess
My mum is six feet under
I am comfortable all the time
I'm cold
I am surround by security
I'm scared
I will live until I'm 100 years old
I'm contemplating suicide
Life is Heaven for high society
Life is Hell for a war orphan.

Luke Rollings (13)
The Rushden Community College

If I Was Given A Voice For The Day

If I was given a voice for the day,
When I'm unable to speak,
I'd like to tell the world how happy I am
And show my true feelings, I would,
To prove how glad I am that the sun is shining,
I'd love to tell my friends,
That oh, I do like to play on the swings,
Also to tell Nichola how much I enjoyed our holiday to America,
I'd have to tell my cousin how much I like her new room
And my sister, how much I like her new clothes,
But if I was given a voice for the day,
When I am unable to speak,
I'd like to say thank you to my mum
And tell my family how I love them so much,
If I was given a voice for the day,
When I am unable to speak!

Sarah Utton (12)
The Rushden Community College

I Wish . . .

Dad's gone, I'm all alone,
No food, no drink, no home,
Two miles to the river, every day,
For dirty water and then I say,
I wish Dad was here.

Then I sleep,
On the street,
When I wake, I scream and shout,
But no one here, the sun's not out,
I hate it in every single way
And then I say,
I wish Dad was here.

Katie Percival (12)
The Rushden Community College

Meaning Of Life

Life in itself is a beautiful thing,
You can dance, love, play, sing,
But what does it all mean in the end,
Knowledge can be a powerful friend.

But life can end in a flash,
Just like that, your life could crash,
Make the most of your life on this Earth,
Have fun all the way, to death through birth.

People go on a quest to find the meaning,
The meaning of life could be so demeaning,
Who, where, what, why?
Fearless people endlessly try,
To find the key to life on Earth,
They will strive to have power.

In the end, it does not matter,
When your life is left in tatters,
The meaning of life, they will never know,
This quest you see can only end
With bodies fed to the crows.

Tom Brogan (12)
The Rushden Community College

The Meaning Of Life

Although life is a blessing,
It can be very depressing,
It comes and goes
And no one knows,
Just what our life will bring.

Life can be bad
And very sad,
But take it in your stride,
Hold your head high with pride,
You're here for the ride!

Joshua Dilley (13)
The Rushden Community College

The Meaning Of Life

The meaning of life is not easy,
So much so, that it makes me queasy,
Sometimes it makes me really low,
But yesterday I realised . . .
I just don't know!

Benjamin James May (13)
The Rushden Community College

Little Labrador

L abraders are very excitable
A ngels, that's what they are
B rown and black are the best colours
R ascals they may be
A lthough they are excitable, they are very cute
D opey and daring that's what they can be
O verall, they are the best dogs
R ump steak is their favourite meal.

Danielle Thomson (11)
The Rushden Community College

My Mummy's Story

My mummy passed away last year,
I cry a river every night,
The tears which run down my colourless face,
Make my despair complete.

She always loved baking cookies with me,
Before she was diagnosed with cancer,
My boogie beat and funky feet,
As I danced all day long with her.

Her beautiful light brunette hair,
Swaying in the gusty breeze,
Oh, how I wish, I wish,
She could be here again.

Louisa Walker (12)
The Rushden Community College

My Grandad

Lots of people die
My grandad had to go
I will love him always
And miss him forever.

I was so sad
When he went
I cried and cried so much
I now sleep in my sorrow
And my tears
Are my blanket.

Kieran O'Connor (11)
The Rushden Community College

When You Entered The World

When you entered the world
I thought how beautiful you were
Roses are red
Violets are blue
Sugar is sweet
And so are you
When you looked at me
I thought
How beautiful thee fits with me.

Keiron Hinde (11)
The Rushden Community College

Pollution

Cars are green,
Lorries are white,
Pollution is bad,
I hope you're glad,
This is all the government's fault,
While we have to face the guilt,
The government gets away scot-free.

Tom Sadler (12)
The Rushden Community College

Rabbits

R abbits love to run about
A nd even hop around
B eautiful and calm
B ut can be grumpy too
I ntelligent they are
T heir teeth are sharp and big
S o, so cute, you can't resist them.

Jessica Norman (11)
The Rushden Community College

Rushden

R ushden is my favourite town
U tterly tasty food
S o come and stay
H omes are good
D inners arc great
E ven now
N othing can beat Rushden.

Paige Kelly (11)
The Rushden Community College

A Hungry Penguin

I waddle around the Antarctic,
Waiting for something to eat,
Oh, how much I wish,
I had a great, big, juicy fish,
All the fish have vanished
From the big blue sea,
I want one for my tea!

I'm getting very hungry,
I think I might starve,
Out here when it's getting dark,
I hope I can survive.

It's getting really dark,
I can feel the breeze,
I'm still very hungry,
I think I'm going to freeze.

But, what's that moving?
Can it be?
Yes, it is,
A great, big, *yummy fish!*

Christopher Taylor (11)
The Rushden Community College

Sheep

Grazing in the green, juicy grass,
Chased by the dog till his fun lasts,
Resting till the night turns to dawn,
We walk about, our feet get stuck on some thorn.

'Baa, baa,' we say to the sheep on the other farm.

Our coats have been shaved,
We're cold in the frost,
We have long, lazy days,
Our wool costs a lot.

'Baa, baa,' we say to the farmer on the farm.

Frances Henman (11)
The Rushden Community College

Grisly Bear

G azing at the stars at night
R elaxing in the caves
I nnocent looks on their faces
S leeping in huddled groups
L ying in the dark
Y oung cubs snuggle up to their mothers

B ut beware, before
E ntering, be very quiet
A nd if you wake them, they will . . .
R oar!

Hollie Wells (12)
The Rushden Community College

Huskies

H andsome as can be
U naware of roads
S tubborn they can be
K een for their food
I deal if you need protecting
E yes of bright blue make them so adorable
S erve them food and they will be happy.

Hannah Clarke (12)
The Rushden Community College

Lena Saunders

L oving, caring and sweet-hearted
E verlasting smile
N ever downhearted
A nd not a bad lump in her heart

S o soft cuddles
A nd church on Sundays
U p in flat 6 she lived
N o one can ever change that
D onations to charity she did
E motions were strong
R ainy days, her smile warms you up
S he would applaud others.

Rhys DeBranco (11)
The Rushden Community College

I Love Dogs

I love dogs,
All breeds of dogs,
Scruffy and fluffy dogs,
Large and small dogs,
Lap dogs,
Top dogs,
Devoted dogs,
Soppy dogs,
Playful dogs,
Aggressive dogs,
Scared dogs,
Happy dogs,
Excited dogs,
Clever dogs,
Lazy dogs,
I love dogs!

Julie Bomben (11)
Wollaston School

People

People, people passing by
Saying hello and then goodbye
Everyone having fun
Underneath the warming sun.

Sarah Welsby (12)
Wollaston School

Snow

It falls softly on the ground
I wake up with such excitement
Happy 'cause there is no school
Cold snowflakes fall on my gloves
Like soft white pillows
It's so cold

Snowballs hit me hard and fast
Like a slap with a fish across my face
Little children making snowmen
All round, snowmen stand proud
Waiting for the boiling sun to take them away
It's winter

A blanket of snow covers the ground
Hiding the danger below
Like a plaster covering a cut
Icicles chime sweetly in the wind
Like the ringing bells of the church
It's snowing.

Charlotte Tennant (13)
Wollaston School

The Abandoned Dog

I lie there in the frosty cold,
My legs and body, bare and bold.
I'm dirty and skinny and no one wants me,
I'm tired and old, but still very cheery.

Ow! My legs and aching feet,
Nothing to be seen on one single street.
I lay there in one big heap,
I stand up, look, cry and weep.

Lewis French (11)
Wollaston School

The Witch's Mansion

In the witch's mansion, there is a sword
It is old, bent and chipped
But it can still fight a thousand fights.

In the witch's mansion, there is a wand
It is dusty, black and old
But the magic is like a flowing river.

In the witch's mansion, there is a potion
It is old, mouldy and smells a lot
But when she gazes into it
It reminds her of all the potions she ever made.

Hannah Tyrer (12)
Wollaston School

Best Friends

James and Henry,
My best friends,
We laugh the day right to the end,
We have lots of fun,
Under the sun,
Playing games until the day is done.

Me and Henry,
Riding our bikes,
Zooming around,
Right through the night.

Me and James
Watching TV,
From BBC,
To ITV.

All together
We have lots of fun,
We're best friends,
My poem is done.

Jacob Thorpe (13)
Wollaston School

What Am I?

I am a butterfly, what am I?
I am a bumblebee, what am I?
I am a dragonfly, what am I?
I am free, that is what I wish, but I am not, not at all
I am really here, stood in a circle of friends, laughing and giggling
Just trying to fit in
I am unable to escape or I will see fists flying towards me
Bad names wiggling out of my friends' mouths
I am a piece of chewing gum, what am I?
I am a pen lid, what am I?
I am the words on a newspaper, what am I?
What I am is stuck, unable to move
Please help!

Wendy Mullaney (11)
Wollaston School

My Favourite Thing To Do

Coming home from school
The best part of the day,
Cos all I want to do
Is sit indoors and play.

My favourite thing of all
I bet you'd never tell,
Is my Xbox games console
That I could never sell!

Disappearing through the TV
I'm a soldier at war,
On 'Call of Duty 3'
I just want to play some more.

I used to like the PlayStation
When that was all the rage,
Games like 'Gran Turismo' were great
When I was half my age.

Long ago, when Dad was a kid
Games were very boring,
Things like 'Space Invaders' and 'Pacman',
(I'd never be a fan)
I'll only end up snoring.

So give me my controllers,
My headset too,
Cos my Xbox games console,
Is my favourite thing to do!

Ryan Herdman-Grant (12)
Wollaston School

In The Old Greenhouse

In the old greenhouse, a mower engine,
Old and rusted, but yet still smells of petrol.
In the old greenhouse, a plant dead and gone,
But the roots still live on.
In the old greenhouse, a panel of shattered glass,
But still as shiny as if new.
In the old greenhouse, a cup, broken,
But still smells of coffee.
In the old greenhouse, a phone, old and gone
But the agonising noise of it ringing lives on.

Matthew West (12)
Wollaston School

The Poem Of I Don't Know!

I don't know what I'm writing
I don't know what to do
I'm stuck, I'm worried
And I haven't got a clue.

I'm starting to panic
My mates are at work
I just want to leave
And never come back.

I just want to miss this exam
But if I do I'm finished
And my life will be a misery
I just want to leave and not look back.

Sam Bolton (13)
Wollaston School

Football Poem

It's the day before the big match
As I open the latch
To the Chelsea changing rooms
Then suddenly, *boom!*
The door slams shut
And all I can hear is a mutt

As I sit and wait in my seat
The entire crowd are eating meat
As I wait for the players to come out
All the lights come on, but no players come out
But then they all shout, 'Where are you Blues?'
I think to myself, *please don't lose!*
But then I go all cold and shape into a mould
My dad shaking me out of the trance
But I just sit and glance
'What?' in a second I'm gone
As I walk away, they sing the National Anthem song
As I'm walking towards the exit
The players come onto the pitch
The crowds are still shouting
As I walk home and go upstairs
I think to myself, *what an outing!*

Emma Roberts (13)
Wollaston School

Mr Gamble

Mr Gamble walks inside the room
I shrink in my chair getting smaller and smaller
I get butterflies in my stomach
As he reaches over me I am scared
He takes the boys report and goes
Thank God he's gone
I sit up and everyone is laughing
The bell rings and off I go again . . .

Amy Millard (11)
Wollaston School

Longtown

In Longtown,
There were no clowns.
We went on a mountain
And looked like a statue on top of a fountain.
Then we went caving,
And now I've got a craving
To go back.
However if you didn't listen, you'd get the sack
We went there with the school,
We had to meet in the café hall.
We all bought our bags
These all had on our name tags
Also when we went, a girl was screaming
And all of a sudden, I heard a heart beating
The teacher who went with us,
Was one we all could trust.
Her name was Miss Reed,
And I'm not sure if she liked swede.
And now I have to go,
So goodbye and ho, ho, ho!

Will Smith (12)
Wollaston School

Me And My Pony, Scruff

Over the fields and far away,
Me and my pony, Scruff, go out to play.
We trot and canter and gallop,
We jump big jumps, small jumps.
We ride all day long,
I love him,
He loves me.
He's cuddly to ride,
He is brown with a black tail and mane
His name is Scruff
We have the sun following us every day.

Fay Wood (11)
Wollaston School

The Deserted House

No glass in the window,
There's no smoke in the chimney,
There's no wood in the fire,
The walls are grey and bare
And the sand lies before their feet,
The house is bent like a broken back,
The tiles are coming off one by one like raindrops,
For some reason, I was not scared,
But then the wind and the rain
Came crashing down on me like a tonne of bricks,
I was running and I looked back for a minute
And I saw something,
But they sparkled and shined and I could not believe my eyes!

Nathan Cruden (11)
Wollaston School

The Cat Poem!

I have two cats,
One called Kizzy,
She is so dizzy,
One called Kiara,
A princess without a tiara,
Kizzy is naughty but nice,
She loves to play with mice,
She loves to bring them in our house,
It's so nice to wake up and find a mouse,
In our house,
Kiara is too posh to push,
We have to open the front door to let her out,
How lush!
Instead of using the cat flap, I have to let her out,
We have to use the front door,
No need to shout,
Kizzy doesn't miaow, she squeaks,
She can't push the cat flap, she is too weak,
All she does is eat
And sleep,
Kiara sits up on the fish tank,
What does she think? *Oh, what a dish!*
My fish looks out with goggle eyes,
What does she think?
My gosh, what a size!
My fish must be scared
Whenever I wake up, I come downstairs,
Kiara and Kizzy glare
I give them food
Then they run upstairs in a good mood
Ready for a day of leisure
Being a cat - what a pleasure!

Lauren Bandey (12)
Wollaston School

A Truly Realised Story

When we got to school, we realised
The walls were down
The lights were damaged
With no one around to see it.

When we got to school, we realised
A big chunk of wall on the floor
And a crow around the door
And not a sign of life to hear it.

When we got to school, we realised
One walkie-talkie, coloured red
With a swift sign of blood going through our heads
Then we said, 'They're dead.'

When we got to school, we realised
A scent of smoke in the air
We turned around, then looked up -
A fiery blaze in front of us
We turned around and ran back to the gate
Before it was too late
Down the street, then down the lane
Then back home where we should stay
Our parents asked us, 'How was school today?'
We said, 'When we got to school, we realised . . .'

Daniel Paine (11)
Wollaston School

The Audition

Oh, my God, I hope I get it,
I've never done an audition before,
Oh, my God, I hope I get it,
Further and further I sing.

I am so nervous, I hope I get it,
Will they like me? I hope they do,
I am so nervous, I hope I get it,
Further and further I sing.

Help, help, I hope I get it,
I hope I don't sing a bad note,
Help, help, I hope I get it,
Further and further I sing.

Oh, my God, I didn't get it,
Oh well, that's how life is,
Oh, my God, I didn't get it,
I will never sing again.

Mathew Leask (12)
Wollaston School

The Commentator

Good afternoon and welcome
This is your commentator, Shaun Turner
Welcoming you to this international hockey match
Between England and Poland.

The carpet looks in brilliant shape
As England's five-time medallist, Daniel, steps in.

The whistle blows, the game begins
Daniel gets the ball and skilfully does an Indian dribble
Past the chair, but what's this?
He's been tackled by the goldfish;
A silly move this -
Flounder no match for him!

He's near the goal, the goal drawing nigh
He shoots . . . he scores!
It's in the net, but it's through the net as well
And it's hit the window!
Mum enters the carpet, she's seen the hole
She's killing Daniel
His Indian dribble won't work on this beast!
He's out, through the door and up the climbing frame
And not holding on.

Dad's home and joins the chase,
Daniel has gone to his room now
The pocket money in his hand
Daniel's out for the month, the year, forever
His stick burnt.

This is Shaun Turner
With the final commentary.

Daniel Bottomley (12) & Shaun Turner (11)
Wollaston School

Bullying!

I sit alone, all alone,
No friends, no feelings,
Just scared and worried.

No one cares, no one likes me
Why do they do it?
Is it hatred? Jealousy?
Is it my personality?

I wish it would stop
I wish I were dead
I want it to stop
I hate them, they hate me.

They beat me, they hurt me
Names, feet, hands, head, fist
That's what they use to hurt me
Why, why, oh why?

Aiden Hornsby (11)
Wollaston School

The Abandoned Dog

I am alone, with no one
They kick me
And punch me
Give me no food
I am alone.

They liked me at first
But then the love went
I am cold and wet
And I need a wash
My coat has gone all saggy.

When I was at the pet shop
There were a lot of dogs
But they chose me
If it was a different dog
Would this have happened
Or is it just me?
I am unwanted with no one to hold me.

The food started off good
But then it got to the cheap food
Lots of people went past
And saw that I had no owner with me
And what did they do?
Nothing!

I sit in the cold
There is a bit of sun
But it is too far away
I can't move
If I do, my legs shake and collapse
So I stay still.

But now that has all changed
I have the good food again
My new family love me
Like Wayne Rooney loves football
And that is a lot!

Daniel Womack (11)
Wollaston School

The Two Kittens

I have two darling kittens, wearing stripy mittens,
The big boy is named Fudge and the small girl is named Toffee,
Neither of them miaow or purr,
Fudge goes *squeak* and Toffee goes *bubble*,
Every time they stare at me, my heart is filled with love,
Their fur is soft and silky, like the finest silk ever made,
Their tails wave round freely, in a little question mark,
Their sweet blue eyes comfort you, when you are worried,
Their paws are warm and tender, with soft, pinky pads,
Both their bodies are cuddly, like the softest teddy bears,
They snuggle up to me at night and give me loving kisses,
I love my little kittens and they love me as well,
They keep trying to catch my animals,
Especially my gerbils, but I love them anyway!

April Addison (11)
Wollaston School

Through The Eyes Of An Abandoned Cat

Here am I, sitting all alone,
Waiting for someone to take me home!

Miaow, miaow - I loudly cry,
As adults and children walk on by.

I silently walk back to my bed
And lay on my blanket where I rest my head.

The doors close to the public, another day in June,
Oh goodness, will I have a new home soon?

Next day, it's an early start
And I'm going to play a very big part.

Here come some new owners, will they pick me?
Could this be the day that I'll be free?

Yes, yes - they're taking me home,
I will be loved forever and never alone!

Ben Nolan (12)
Wollaston School

Bobby Moore

Through the eyes of Bobby Moore
Who played football and loved to score.
He played for West Ham and England
Against teams throughout all the land.
Captain of both the teams he played in
A man who didn't like to lose, but to win.
He lifted many trophies and cups
The one most famous - summer of '66.
Played at the home of football - Wembley
When he was lifted aloft, he smiled with glee
This is a hero to me, Bobby Moore MBE.

Thomas Williams (11)
Wollaston School

Dance X

All you can hear is your heart beating
And the crowd clapping to the tune
Knowing that you're on stage soon
But the feeling that's in my belly
Makes my legs go like jelly
I don't think I can do it
But I know my mates will get me through it
Now the time has come
I've got to go on and dance to a stupid song
I feel so happy, now I'm on stage
Having fun with my mates
When you come off stage
The feeling is great!

Sarah Jones (12)
Wollaston School

The Abandoned School

In a dark, old building, creaky and damp
Hanging on the side, a broken lamp
Years ago, it used to be a school
On the left, a dark, dirty pool

Seeing figures of misty ghosts
Ash remains from bags and coats
Nobody is here, this place is forgotten
Everything here is going rotten

Continuous rain beats on the ground
All you can hear, is a howling sound
Nobody knows the real truth
Untold secrets, held under that roof.

Leah Galea-Bateman (13)
Wollaston School

Pirates

'Yo, ho, a pirate's life for me!'
Wooden leg, thief and crook
Eye patch, gold and handy hook
Captain's parrot, rum and crew
Walk the plank, 'The depths for you!'
Compass, treasure, travel the sea
Here's the map, where's the key?
Scimitars, cannons and cabin boy
Islands, sharks, 'There be land ahoy!'
'Yo, ho, a pirate's life for me!'

Joanna Morton (12)
Wollaston School

The Abused Dog

I lay there in almighty pain
All the other kids in the passing lane
Just stand there and stare
My abusers come and slam me into the car
They speed off with me
It seems like we have travelled very far
The brakes slam on and we skid round
They get out of the car and give me a pound
I yelp
They shout at me, saying, 'Get out! Get out!'
I look round, all I can see is water and boats
Wiggling up and down
They throw me, I land in freezing water
And all I can hear are the laughs and giggles
Of my tormentors.

Kyle Adams (13)
Wollaston School

My Cat!

I have this cat
And it's really fat,
It goes and sits on my mat,
It also stares at my rat.

My cat is blue, like the sky,
Also a bit shy,
She loves pie,
Then she goes to sleep with a sigh.

She hates going for fresh air,
Me and her make a good pair
And we like to share,
Also we both care.

Stacey Cooper (13)
Wollaston School

Ladybirds And Spiders

Ladybirds are small
They're not very tall
They're red with black spots
Or yellow with black dots

Spiders are scary
Some are hairy
Spiders are black
Poisonous ones attack.

Ashleigh Stroud (13)
Wollaston School

Me And You

I'm the ball,
I'm the life,
I'm the colour and the light,
I'm the day and the night,
I'm the sea and the land.

What can I be?
You see me all the time
But sometimes you never see me at all
You take me for granted
You pollute me every day
But be careful, I might not be here to stay.

Take care, be wise,
So tomorrow never dies,
Don't pollute me with your poisons,
Let's work together,
So we last forever!

Sarah Priscott (12)
Wollaston School

The Castle

The night before, I was sure
I was going on stage at the castle.
The big day had come
For my dad and mum
Who sat in the stalls at the castle.
We took our positions
And like kids on a mission
We danced our hearts out
On the stage at the castle.
The time went like a flash
It was a box office smash
And we enjoyed ourselves
On stage at the castle.

Samantha Gould (12)
Wollaston School

Young Writers Information

We hope you have enjoyed reading this book - and that you will continue to enjoy it in the coming years.

If you like reading and writing poetry drop us a line, or give us a call, and we'll send you a free information pack.

Alternatively if you would like to order further copies of this book or any of our other titles, then please give us a call or log onto our website at
www.youngwriters.co.uk

Young Writers Information
Remus House
Coltsfoot Drive
Peterborough
PE2 9JX

(01733) 890066